Beautiful Words

A Dictionary

David Tuffley

To my beloved Nation of Four
Concordia Domi – Foris Pax

Language... has created the word "loneliness" to express the pain of being alone. And it has created the word "solitude" to express the glory of being alone -- Paul Tillich.

Published 2012 by Altiora Publications
AltioraPublications.com/
ISBN-13: 978-1477529089 ISBN-10: 147752908X

About the Author
David Tuffley PhD has had a consuming interest in language since books became his best earthly companions as a child in growing up in pre-computer world.

Acknowledgements
Special thanks are due to my partner Angela for her unwavering support and encouragement.

Introduction

As English has evolved over the past 1,500 years, words that were once in common usage have slipped out of usage. Some are delightful, others not so much. This book blows the dust off over a thousand delightful words, bringing them to a whole new audience. If you enjoy words for their own sake, or if you are at all curious about how people talked and wrote when the world was a quite different place, then this book is for you. The perfect gift for those who love words.

Ever since it emerged as a distinct language from the West Germanic dialect spoken by early arrivals to what is now called England around the 5th Century C.E, English has busily absorbed many thousands of words from Ancient Greek, Roman Latin, the Northern Germanic languages of Scandinavia, the French spoken in Normandy, and more recently from countries that were once part of the British Empire (for example India). Most recently, American English has contributed many words to colourfully describe the modern world. The *Oxford English Dictionary* in 2011 lists over 250,000 words, and that does not include many more technical and slang words.

Use this book like a hungry person would approach a delicious buffet lunch. It deserves to be consumed slowly, savouring the flavours and giving them time to be properly digested.

A

Absinthe: a green, highly alcoholic (45–74% ABV / 90-148 proof) anise flavoured liquor.

Acciaccatura: an ornamental note, one half step or one whole step below a principal note.

Acedia: a state of listless boredom, spiritual apathy.

Acervuline: aggregated, heaped up, localized.

Acidulous: sour to the taste, acidic of manner, sarcastic.

Acolyte: junior member of clergy, an assistant in liturgical proceedings.

Acquiesce: passive acceptance of what is.

Adroit: skilful and fast in action or thought.

Adumbrate: explain something in vague terms.

Aeipathy: on-going passion, continuing disease.

Aeneous: golden-green colour.

Aeolian: like the wind.

Aeonian: eternal.

Aerial: relating to the air.

Aesthete: an appreciator of art or beauty.

Aestival: relating to Summer.

Aeviternal: eternal.

Afflatus: creative inspiration.

Aileron: movable control surface on trailing edge of aircraft wing.

Ailurophile: cat-lover.

Alabaster: translucent, mostly white stone (made from gypsum).

Alienate: to make someone hostile or unfriendly.

Aliment: food, sustenance.

Allegretto: moderately fast tempo.

Alleviate: to lessen the unpleasant effects of something.

Alloquy: to speak to another person.

Allure: attraction.

Alluvium: sediment at bottom of river or sear.

Amaranth: purple flower, a metaphor for immortality.

Amber: yellowy-brown colour.

Ambience: the atmosphere or feeling of a place.

Ambivalence: conflicted feelings.

Ambrosia: absolutely delicious food (of the gods).

Ameliorate: to improve.

Amelus: a person with missing limbs.

Amethyst: gemstone (deep purple).

Amnesia: loss of memory.

Amorphous: without shape.

Amphisbaena: two-headed snake (Greek mythology).

Amphora: two-handled vase with a narrow neck, common in Classical Greece.

Amulet: good luck charm, protection against misfortune.

Analemma: figure-8 showing sun's path.

Ancestry: the line of progenitors from which someone descends.

Andante: moderately slow (in music).

Anemone: marine creature with flower-like tentacles.

Antebellum: before the war.

Anxiolytic: lessening of anxiety, a tranquilizer.

Aperitif: drink taken before a meal to stimulate the appetite.

Aphelion: orbit of earth when furthest from the sun.

Aphesis: omission of sound at beginning of a word or phrase.

Aphotic: no light.

Apocope: omission of sound at end of a word or phrase..

Apophenia: belief in causal relationship between unrelated events.

Apoplexy: stroke (cerebral haemorrhage).

Aposiopesis: abrupt halt to a train of thought or speech.

Apostasy: abandonment of one's faith or principles.

Apostolicity: contemporary of the Apostles.

Apotheosis: achieving divine status.

Apropos: appropriate.

Aquarelle: transparent watercolour technique.

Aqueous: relating to water.

Aquiline: relating to an eagle's beak.

Arabesque: ballet move involving rotation.

Aria: operatic solo song.

Artemisia: aromatic shrub.

Ascertain: to determine the facts.

Ashlar: a block of building stone smoothed to face outwards.

Asphodel: flower from the underworld.

Assemblage: a gathering.

Astral: relating to the stars.

Asylum: a place of refuge, to restore sanity or enable recovery.

Atelier: artist's studio.

Athanasy: deathless, immortal.

Athenaeum: institution for literary or scientific learning.

Aubade: poem or song relating to the dawn or morning.

Auburn: reddish-brown, most often relating to hair.

Aura: the subtle surrounding energy of a person or thing.

Austere: making do with very little.

Autumnal: relating to Autumn.

Auxiliary: something held in reserve.

Avarice: greed, particularly for money.

Avenue: handsome, wide street, often lined with trees.

Azalea: garden flower.

Azoth: a universal solvent.

Azuline: light blue.

Azure: sky blue.

B

Baccalaureate: undergraduate university degree.

Balustrade: architectural element on a building that prevents people from falling.

Banderilla: in bullfighting, the dart shot into the bull's neck to weaken and enrage him.

Bardiglio: fine grained Italian marble.

Basilica: a Roman public building later converted to a church.

Bastille: infamous former prison in Paris.

Bayonet: a stabbing weapon fitted to the muzzle end of a rifle.

Beleaguer: to exhaust through repeated attack.

Belladonna: toxic plant.

Belle-lettres: beautiful writing, as opposed to practical writing.

Bellicose: ready to fight.

Bellwether: an opinion-leader.

Belvedere: a roofed observation tower attached to a building.

Berceuse: lullaby.

Bethesda: a holy place.

Bezaleel: the shadow of God.

Bibelot: a small, valuable trinket.

Bibliophile: book-lover.

Bijouterie: a collection or display of trinkets or jewels.

Bivouac: temporary military camp.

Blaze: brightly burning fire.

Blellum: a loud gossiper.

Bliss: great happiness.

Blithe: happy and carefree.

Blossom: a flower, or process of flowering.

Bloviate: pompous talk.

Boeotian: crude, ignorant behavior.

Borasca: a brief storm, usually with thunder and lightning.

Bordereau: detailed statement of account.

Boulevard: a broad, handsome street.

Bouleversement: sudden reversal (of fortune).

Bourgeoisie: the middle class in Marxist ideology.

Braggadocio: arrogant, boastful person.

Brecciate: rock composed of sharp fragments set in a finer matrix.

Breeze: gentle wind.

Breviloquence: brief speech.

Brevity: briefness.

Bricolage: improvised construction using materials readily to hand.

Brio: high spirited.

Brood: to sulk, think darkly.

Bucolic: relating to beautiful countryside, Nature.

Bungalow: a snug cottage.

Burnish: to polish.

C

Caballero: an expert horseman, gentleman.

Cabaret: live entertainment venue, often with dining.

Cadence: the rhythm of language or music.

Cadenza: improvised musical or literary composition.

Caesious: blue/gray.

Caesura: a literary pause.

Calico: plain-woven textile made from unbleached cotton.

Caliginous: dark, difficult to distinguish in the gloom.

Calliope: a steam powered whistle organ operated from a keyboard.

Callipygian: a beautiful bottom (on a person).

Callow: inexperienced person, often immature.

Calypso: a dance originating in the West Indies.

Cancrizans: rear-wards movement.

Candelabra: a multi-branched candlestick holder.

Canticle: a song by a church choir.

Capriccio: improvised composition, not governed by rules.

Capricious: foolishly impulsive.

Caress: loving touch, stroke.

Cartesian: relating to French philosopher Rene Descartes.

Cascarilla: aromatic West Indian shrub.

Catena: linked series, usually of writing.

Cathismata: one of 20 divisions in a Greek Psalter.

Cavil: to object on trivial grounds.

Cedilla: diacritic character to change pronunciation "façade".

Celadon: light green.

Celeripedean: fleet of foot, a fast runner.

Celerity: with quick enthusiasm.

Celesta: musical instrument.

Celestial: of heaven.

Cello: stringed wooden instrument same shape as a violin, but larger.

Cellophane: clear wrapping paper made from cellulose.

Cellular: relating to cells.

Cellulite: dimpled flesh.

Celluloid: transparent material used to manufacture photographic film.

Cenotaph: a war memorial or empty tomb for soldiers buried elsewhere.

Centennial: every 100 years.

Cerulean: watery blue.

Cerumen: ear-wax.

Cessation: pause, ending.

Chalice: sacred drinking vessel.

Chamois: fine-grained leather from antelope of same name.

Champagne: sparkling white wine from Champagne region of France.

Chandelier: ornate glass light fitting suspended from ceiling.

Chantpleure: to sing and cry simultaneously.

Chariot: horse-drawn military or ceremonial vehicle.

Chartreuse: vivid green used in high visibility clothing.

Chatelaine: lady in charge of a large household.

Chatoyant: resembling a cat's eye.

Chauffeur: the servant who drives a vehicle for their employer.

Cheilion: corner of the mouth.

Chevelure: a full head of hair.

Chiaroscuro: strongly contrasting composition of light and dark.

Chiasmus: inverse rhetorical device, i.e. "eat to live, not live to eat".

Choreography: arrangement of movement on stage.

Cicada: locust-like insect that makes a loud chirruping noise.

Cinder: fully burned, not capable of further burning.

Cinnabar: bright red.

Cinquefoil: plant with five-leaves.

Circlet: ring-shaped ornament or jewellery.

Circuitous: circular, as in an indirect route.

Cislunar: the space between earth and the moon.

Cistern: underground reservoir, usually holding water.

Citadel: safe fortress.

Cithara: a lyre (musical instrument).

Civility: politeness.

Clandestine: secretive deeds, often done under cover of darkness.

Clarion: trumpet with loud piercing note.

Clavicle: collarbone.

Clavilux: light-show linked to music.

Clemency: mercy.

Clerisy: the educated class in society.

Clinquant: glittering with gold colour.

Clithridiate: like a keyhole.

Cloister: the covered, often arched walkway of a monastery.

Coalesce: to join or fuse together.

Coelacanth: an species of ancient fish, a so-called 'living fossil'.

Coercion: to forcibly persuade.

Collectanea: collected writings of an author or authors.

Colliquate: to liquefy.

Colloquial: informal speech or writing, slang.

Colophon: emblem on a book.

Coloratura: elaborate vocal music.

Comestibles: food.

Communiqué: an official announcement.

Conciliabule: a meeting of conspirators.

Conciliate: to persuade someone from hostility to amity.

Concinnity: harmony of the parts with the whole.

Concupiscence: lascivious, lustful.

Congelifraction: splitting rocks by freezing the water in them.

Constellation: arrangement of stars.

Convalesce: to recover from serious injury or illness.

Copse: small forest.

Coquelicot: red poppy.

Coquette: flirtatious woman.

Coracle: circular boat made from skins stretched across a frame.

Cordillera: a mountain range forming part of a larger chain of mountains.

Coriander: aromatic herb.

Corinthian: pertaining to Corinth.

Cortical: relating to cortex.

Coruscate: sparkle, shimmer.

Cosmology: the study of the physical universe.

Cosmopolitan: pertaining to the larger world.

Coterie: a small group united by a common purpose.

Cotillion: An 18th century dance of French origin.

Craquelure: the network of cracks on the surface of old paintings.

Crescendo: gradual increase of tempo or volume (of music).

Crystal: multi-facetted gem-like mineral formation.

Cumulonimbus: billowing cloud.

Cuneiform: an early form of clay-tablet writing.

Curlicue: a fancy flourish in hand-writing.

Cursive: connected hand-writing, sometimes called running writing.

Cuvette: tubular laboratory vessel.

Cyan: green/blue.

Cyaneous: deep blue.

Cygnet: immature swan.

Cylinder: a cylindrical tube.

Cymbal: percussive instrument.

Cynophilist: dog-lover.

Cynosure: the focus of attraction.

Cypress: variety of tree, often growing in swampy areas.

Cytherean: of great beauty, pertaining to the goddess Aphrodite.

Czigany: gypsy, Romani.

D

Daedalian: intelligent, pertaining to Daedalus.

Dalliance: a romantic interlude.

Daphnean: shy, timid.

Dapple: mottles markings, often in clusters.

Dawn: sunrise, enlightenment.

Decrescendo: lowering of tempo in music.

Degringolade: a sharp decline in strength or condition.

Deign: to condescend.

Delenda: to be deleted or which already been deleted.

Delineate: to trace the boundaries, to explain.

Deliquesce: to dissolve.

Delirium: state of irrationality due to high fever.

Delitescent: concealed.

Dell: a pleasant valley, usually small and wooded.

Delphic: pertaining to the Oracle of Delphi.

Demarche: course of action.

Demesne: a lord's domain.

Demure: shy, modest in demeanour.

Denouement: final resolution of a dramatic plot.

Desuetude: disused, useless.

Desultory: slow.

Diablerie: pertaining to the devil, witchcraft, sorcery.

Diaphanous: translucent.

Diaspora: scattering to the four winds.

Dissemble: deceive.

Dilettante: a hobbyist of no great commitment.

Dioscuric: pertaining to twins or duplicates.

Dissemble: to conceal or mislead.

Dissimulate: to conceal with intent to deceive.

Divisi: divided, separated (of music).

Dulcet: sweet to the ear.

Dulciloquy: sweet words.

Dulcimer: stringed instrument with three or four strings.

Dulcinea: a loved one.

Dyslexia: when word order becomes confused.

E

Ebon: black or very dark brown (as in the wood ebony).

Ebullient: high-spirited, enthusiastic.

Echelon: level in a hierarchy.

Echo: a repeated sound, caused by reflection off a hard surface.

Echolalia: repetition of words spoken by others.

Eclipsareon: a machine for viewing eclipses (of the sun, moon etc).

Eclipse: when something becomes obscured by another body positioned in front of it.

Effervesce: bubbly.

Effleurage: smooth, rhythmic stroke employed in massage.

Efflorescence: flowers coming into bloom.

Effluvium: a liquid discharge, often of a disgusting nature.

Efflux: an outward flow of some liquid.

Effulgent: brightly shining, sometimes shimmering.

Effusive: excessive outward flow.

Eglantine: variety of European rose.

Eiderdown: the soft under feathers of the eider duck, used for stuffing pillows and quilts.

Eidolon: a persistent ghostly image.

Élan: high spirited, enthusiastic.

Elapse: to pass by, to finish.

Elasticity: the ability to return to its original shape after stretching.

Elation: a feeling of happiness.

Eleemosynary: being reliant on charity, to make a charitable donation.

Element: a fundamental constituent in the make-up of a larger entity.

Eleven: the number following ten.

Elicit: to draw out of.

Elision: the dropping of a sound from a pronounced word (e.g. man 'o war).

Elixir: a health tonic with alcohol as an important ingredient.

Ellipsis: a missing word or phrase necessary for correct syntax.

Elliptical: in the shape of an ellipse (e.g. oval-shaped).

Eloign: to carry something away and conceal it (e.g. buried treasure).

Eloquence: well-articulated speech.

Elucidate: to clarify.

Elusive: difficult to catch or hold on to.

Elysian: pertaining to the Elysian Fields (e.g. heaven).

Elysium: place where heroes go when they die.

Emaciate: to become excessively thin, as in a wasting disease.

Emanation: something issuing forth from a source, like a ray of light.

Embarcadero: a landing where boats may unload passengers and goods.

Ember: slowly burning piece of wood or coal, with little or no flame.

Embrocation: apply lotion to the skin.

Emerald: dark green gemstone.

Emissary: a messenger sent ahead to prepare for the arrival of an important person.

Emission: a discharge (e.g. of light).

Emollient: skin moisturiser.

Empyreal: celestial.

Emulate: to imitate.

Emulsify: to blend two or more non-soluble liquids to form an emulsion (e.g. oil and water).

Enamel: a hard, usually opaque glass-like outer finish.

Enceinte: pregnant, or the fortifications of a castle.

Encomium: excessive praise for another, usually in a formal setting.

Enhalo: to encircle with a halo.

Ennui: boredom, discontent.

Ensconce: to settle in to a safe comfortable place.

Epée: a blunt-edged sword used in the sport of fencing.

Epergne: centre-piece of a table.

Ephebe: young man.

Ephemeral: brief.

Epicede: funeral song.

Epicurean: one who enjoys the sensual pleasures of life in all its forms.

Epigone: an inferior imitator.

Epileptic: pertaining to epilepsy.

Epiphany: a sudden realisation or awakening.

Epistle: a letter, usually formal.

Epitaph: the inscription on a gravestone.

Epithelium: skin of the body.

Epitome: a perfect example.

Equestrian: relating to horse-riding.

Equinox: when day and night are of equal duration, happens twice a year.

Equipoise: balanced, poised.

Eristic: where a person argues over small, often deceptive points.

Erstwhile: at an earlier time, former.

Escadrille: a squadron of six (ships, planes etc).

Escalade: climbing a precipice with ladder or rope.

Escamotage: sleight of hand, as in magic tricks.

Escarole: green chicory.

Esclavage: a necklace with multiple rows or layers.

Escritoire: writing desk.

Esculent: safe to eat.

Esoterica: an item that is rare or with obscure meaning.

Esper: a person with psychic abilities.

Esprit: spirit.

Essence: the indispensable element(s) of something that characterise it.

Esssse: plural of ashes.

Estuary: the zone where a river meets the sea/ocean.

Esurient: hungry.

Ethereal: insubstantial, translucent.

Etiolate: to inhibit growth by keeping away from the sun.

Etude: a piece of music played by students learning the instrument.

Eunoia: good mental health.

Euphonious: good-sounding.

Euphoria: feeling of bliss, great happiness.

Evanescent: brief, not lasting long.

Evaporation: turning from liquid to vapour.

Eviscerate: to disembowel.

Evocative: that which evokes, something that reminds, inspires, or impresses.

Excelsior: curled wood shavings.

Exclusion: the act of excluding.

Existential: relating to existence.

Expatiate: to speak or write at some length and detail.

Exuviate: to moult.

F

Façade: the outward face shown to the world that conceals what lies behind it.

Facility: a functional building that serves a purpose, or a particular skill.

Facsimile: a copy or reproduction.

Fainéant: a lazy person, often dishonest.

Falciform: convex curve.

Famished: ravenously hungry.

Famulus: a sorcerer's assistant.

Felicity: happiness.

Fetching: attractive, pretty, usually in relation to women.

Fiasco: a confused situation.

Fissure: a narrow often jagged crack (e.g. in rock or glacial ice).

Fleur-de-lys: a three leaved insignia based on the lily.

Foliage: the green leaves of a tree or shrub.

Forbearance: not reacting to provocation.

Formulaic: the standard, formula-driven way.

Forte: the specialty that someone excels at.

Foudroyant: a sudden display of dazzling intensity.

Frescade: a pleasant shady place to walk or rest.

Frolic: playful action.

Frost: frozen dew.

Fuchsia: vivid pinkish-purple.

Fugacious: short-lived, fleeting.

Fuliginous: a dark, dirty colour, like coal-soot.

Fumarole: a volcanic vent from which vapour escapes.

Fumulus: thin cloud, like a veil.

Furrow: a groove dug in the earth suitable for planting seeds.

Fuselage: the body of an aeroplane to which the wings attach.

Fusillade: a volley of gun-fire.

G

Galaxy: a coherent collection of billions of stars and planets.

Gale: very strong wind.

Galleria: a long room or mall with high, vaulted ceiling.

Gallery: a mezzanine observation area in a public building.

Gambol: to playfully leap.

Gaucherie: embarrassingly awkward.

Girandole: a mirror illuminated by candles fixed to either side.

Glacial: slow but inexorable, like the flow of a glacier.

Glamour: beauty, attractive in a showy way.

Glimpse: brief glance.

Glisten: to shine or glisten.

Gloaming: the period after sunset but before fully dark.

Gloom: sadness.

Glyph: a writing character with specific meaning.

Gossamer: spider's web.

Gracile: gracefully slender.

Grandeur: impressively grand in stature.

Grazioso: graceful, smooth, or elegant in style (musical term).

H

Hacienda: the big house on a farm or ranch where the owner lives.

Halcyon: mythical bird that nests on the calm waters.

Hallucinate: images generated by the mind rather than received via the senses.

Harbinger: messenger of future events.

Hazel: light brown or pale yellow.

Heath: unused land not suitable for cultivation.

Hegemony: the dominant influence.

Heliotrope: a flower that follows the light.

Helix: a spiral.

Henna: reddish-brown dye used cosmetically.

Hubris: excessive pride.

Hue: shade of colour.

Humiliate: to diminish a person's self-esteem.

Hyacinth: a herb, or reddish gem-stone.

I

Icicle: a sliver of frozen water.

Idyllic: an ideal situation, very pleasant.

Ilium: the joint where the femur (leg-bone) meets the pelvis.

Illusion: seeing something that is not physically there.

Illusory: like an illusion.

Illustrate: to clarify with a picture or example.

Imbrication: regular pattern with over-lapping elements.

Imbroglio: a fiasco, a confused situation.

Imbue: to invest with a quality.

Immaculate: without stain or impurity.

Immure: to contain within walls.

Impedimenta: obstructions.

Impetus: movement backed by considerable momentum.

Impluvium: pool in the atrium of Roman house.

Imprimatur: official seal of approval.

Incalescent: becoming hotter.

Incarnadine: the colour of flesh.

Incense: to enrage; aromatic spice for ceremonial burning.

Incipient: at the beginning.

Incisive: cutting through.

Incunabula: books printed prior to 1501.

Indolent: lazy.

Ineffable: impossible to describe in words.

Inertia: a body continues in its existing state of rest or uniform motion.

Influenza: severe viral infection of the respiratory tract.

Ingénue: an innocent girl or young woman.

Inglenook: a cosy fireplace hearth.

Ingravescent: slowly becoming more severe.

Innocent: without guilt.

Inoccuity: harmless.

Inoculate: to inject an idea into a person's mind, or vaccine into the body.

Insipid: mild, lacking in flavour.

Insouciance: nonchalance.

Intaglio: figure carved into stone or wood.

Inundate: to submerge.

Inure: to become accustomed.

Iris: the coloured part of the eye around the pupil.

Iscariotic: traitorous.

Isinglass: translucent mica.

Isosceles: a kind triangle having two equal sides.

Isthmus: strip of land connecting two larger land masses.

Ivory: elephant tusk.

J

Jacqueminot: scarlet rose.

Jaunt: a brief pleasure trip.

Jejune: naïve.

Kaleidoscope: an optical tube with internal mirrors to create symmetrical images.

K

Kismet: fate.

Knell: solemn bell-ringing.

L

L'esprit de l'escalier: "staircase wit" or thinking of a great comeback too late.

Labial: pertaining to lips.

Labyrinth: maze.

Lacerate: to cut.

Laconic: saying little, and doing so rather slowly.

Lacquer: varnish that dries to a glossy finish.

Lacuna: gap.

Lagniappe: reward for loyal customer; special gift.

Lagoon: a shallow, inshore body of water.

Lambent: glowing with soft radiance.

Laminate: to create multiple bonded layers.

Languid: listless.

Languorous: moving in a slow, relaxed manner.

Laodicean: having no strong opinion in important matters.

Lapis Lazuli: vivid blue gemstone.

Largesse: generous gift-giving.

Lascivious: lustful.

Lassitude: tiredness.

Lathe: tool for the shaping wood by high-speed rotation.

Lattice: cross-hatched panel.

Lavadero: laundry.

Lavender: pale purple.

Lavish: giving in generous amounts.

Layer: single thickness covering a surface.

Legerity: mental sharpness.

Leisure: free time.

Leitmotif: recurrent musical theme.

Lemniscate: figure-eight symbol.

Lemonade: non-alcoholic drink made from lemon juice, sugar, and water.

Lesbian: homosexual female.

Lethe: torpor.

Leveret: a young rabbit.

Leviathan: gigantic creature.

Levitation: when an object rises with no apparent support.

Lexiphanes: person who pretentiously displays their vocabulary.

Liaison: having relations with, either at a personal, social or business level.

Libeccio: South-westerly wind in Corsica, Italy.

Lilliputian: very small.

Lilt: a pleasing rhythm and melody to a way of speaking.

Limerence: long-term infatuation.

Limn: to illustrate with words or pictures.

Limousine: a luxurious passenger vehicle, driven by a chauffeur.

Limpid: the appearance of a deep, clear body of water.

Lineaments: tracing the essential features of something.

Linguistics: the study of languages.

Linoleum: durable, water-proof floor covering.

Liquid: as in solid, liquid, gas.

Lissom: supple, flexible, as in a young woman.

Listless: lethargic.

Litany: large quantity.

Literati: educated people.

Lithe: having a willowy grace, flexible.

Lithium: highly-reactive element in same family as Sodium.

Lithosphere: outermost layer of a planet.

Litterateur: a lover of literature.

Lixiviation: separating the soluble from insoluble.

Lochetic: stealthily waiting for prey.

Loom: used for weaving; or an object coming into view.

Loquacious: talkative.

Lorgnette: a pair of spectacles with a handle to hold them in place.

Lubricious: oily, intentionally lewd.

Lucent: shining.

Lugubrious: gloomy.

Lullaby: bed-time song for children.

Luminal: the perception of light.

Luminary: one who shines, as in an outstanding person in their field.

Lunacy: insanity, as in lunatic.

Lunula: the white part at the base of the fingernail.

Luscious: delicious, juicy.

Lustrous: shiny, glowing.

M

Macedoine: medley of diced fruit or vegetables.

Magisterial: having the dignified bearing of a master, or teacher.

Malady: sickness.

Malaise: generalised sense of being unwell.

Malapropos: inappropriate.

Malleable: easily shaped, usually with the hands.

Mannequin: a dress-makers' dummy.

Mantelletta: sleeveless, knee-length vestment worn by Catholic clergy.

Maquette: scale model.

Maraschino: cordial made from marasca cherries.

Marasmus: a wasting illness.

Marble: decorative stone used in building and statuary.

Marcescent: a withered flower that remains intact.

Marginalia: notes written in the margins of a book.

Marionette: a puppet.

Marmalade: citrus jam.

Marmoreal: made of marble.

Masquerade: festivities involving the wearing of masks.

Material: a physical substance.

Matriculate: to meet the admission standards of a university or other.

Matutinal: early in the morning.

Maudlin: sadly sentimental.

Mausoleum: a stately building containing multiple tombs.

Mauve: pink-purple.

Medallion: a medal or amulet worn around the neck.

Medley: a tasteful mixture of diverse elements.

Melisma: extending a syllable across several notes.

Mellifluous: honey-like.

Mellisonant: sweet-sounding.

Melody: a pleasing pattern of notes.

Memento: a remembrance, an object of personal significance.

Memorabilia: various significant items worthy of keeping.

Menagerie: a zoo.

Meniscus: the curved surface of liquid formed by surface tension.

Mephitic: foul-smelling, possibly poisonous.

Mercurial: fluidly changeable in manner, like mercury.

Mere: of little importance or consequence.

Meretricious: gaudy outward show but with little actual substance.

Meridian: noon; a line drawn from North pole to South pole.

Mestizo: having mixed heritage of American Indian and European.

Métier: a person's particular strength or specialty.

Mewl: soft whimpering sound, like a kitten.

Mezzanine: intermediate level above the ground floor.

Miasma: noxious smell, unhealthy odour.

Mica: a mineral that separates into thin sheets.

Midst: middle.

Mien: attitude expressed by person.

Milieu: the general environment, the atmosphere of a place.

Millennium: one thousand years.

Milquetoast: timid person.

Mimesis: imitation.

Mimosa: the wattle tree.

Mimsy: insubstantial; or great skill.

Miniscule: very small.

Minutiae: the fine detail.

Mirror: a reflective surface.

Miscellany: various objects.

Mist: vapour, most often water vapour as fog.

Mithril: a fictional steel alloy used in weaponry.

Mizzenmast: the mast behind the mainmast on a ship having 3 or more masts.

Mizzle: fine drizzling rain.

Moiety: one of two halves.

Mondigreen: to mishear something.

Morceau: literary or musical composition.

Mormorando: with a murmuring sound.

Moue: pouting face.

Murmur: low, indistinct voice or sound.

Myriad: a large number of.

Myrrh: fragrant resin used in incense and perfume.

Mystique: the special skill needed to excel at an activity.

Mythopoeic: myth-making.

N

Nacreous: having the appearance of mother-of-pearl.

Naiad: a nature spirit that lives near water.

Naïveté: blissful ignorance.

Nebulae: gaseous clouds.

Nemesis: implacable enemy.

Nenuphar: water lily.

Neophyte: a beginner.

Nepenthe: a drug that makes you forget your problems.

Nepheliad: a nature spirit that lives in the clouds.

Nephew: the son of a brother or sister in relation to you.

Nickelodeon: theatre charging five cents entry.

Nimbus: rain clouds.

Nimiety: overabundance.

Nirvana: heaven, a place with no suffering.

Niveous: snow-like.

Nocive: toxic, dangerous.

Noctilucence: illuminated clouds in the night-sky.

Nonchalant: casual, indifferent.

Novae: star in the process of self-destruction.

Novella: short piece of writing.

Novitiate: novice, beginner.

Nucleus: the centre around which other parts are grouped.

Nugacious: trivial.

Nullibicity: non-existence.

Nullifidian: a person with no faith or beliefs.

Numeral: a number.

Numina: divine spirit of place, creative genius.

Numinous: the feeling of being in the presence of the divine.

Numismatics: the pastime of collecting coins and bank-notes.

Nymph: a sexy woman; or a nature spirit in female form.

Nymphet: young, sexually attractive girl.

O

Oasis: water-hole and surrounding foliage in a desert.

Objet d'art: object of art.

Oblivion: completely gone and forgotten.

Obsequious: sycophantic.

Obsidian: black volcanic glass, used for ceremonial knives.

Ocelot: wild cat, similar appearance to leopard only smaller.

Odalisque: female servant.

Oeillade: a flirtatious glance.

Oeuvre: an artist's body of work.

Offing: the sea way off towards the horizon.

Oleander: ornamental shrub with beautiful though poisonous flowers.

Onomatopoeia: a word that sounds like the thing it describes.

Opacity: opaqueness.

Opalescent: having the shimmering colours of opal.

Opaque: not transparent to light.

Ophidian: relating to snakes.

Opulence: wealth.

Opusculum: lesser work of literature.

Orbital: relating to an orbit, as in sun, moon etc.

Orchestra: group of musician playing in concert with each other.

Oscillate: to swing back and forth, like a pendulum.

Ossuary: repository for bones, as in relics of saints kept in churches.

Otiose: indolent, lazy.

Oubliette: well-like dungeon, accessible only from above.

P

Palatial: like a palace.

Palaver: lots of talk that is ultimately quite meaningless.

Palimpsest: recycled parchment/canvass, old content is erased to make room for new.

Palisade: a fence or fortified barrier of stakes set in the ground.

Palladian: relating to Goddess Athena, or architect Andrea Palladio.

Palliasse: crude mattress stuffed with straw or similar.

Palliate: to ease pain or suffering.

Pallid: pale.

Panacea: a medicinal cure-all.

Panoply: a complete set, full array.

Panoramic: a broad view of a scene.

Pantomime: version of theatre with no dialogue only gestures.

Parabola: a curved shape similar to a headlight reflector.

Paradigm: a standard set of theories and beliefs.

Paramour: lover, particularly in an extra-marital sense.

Paraph: an elaborate flourish in a signature.

Paroxysm: a sudden attack, or seizure.

Parvenu: a person who aspires or pretends to be of a higher social class.

Pasquinade: satirical work.

Pastiche: art that is a patchwork of pre-existing elements.

Patina: natural oxidation on metallic surface that increases with age.

Patois: uneducated language.

Paucity: scarcity.

Peccadillo: a small mistake or sin.

Peccavi: confession to a crime or misdemeanour.

Pellucid: having a transcendent clarity.

Peninsula: a finger –like projection of land into the ocean.

Pensive: thoughtful.

Penumbra: partial shadow.

Percolate: liquid soaking through a filter medium, like rain soaking into the earth.

Perennial: lasting the whole year.

Perforate: to pierce with holes.

Periphery: the boundary, or out limits.

Permeate: to extend throughout.

Perpetuity: forever, without end.

Phantasm: something seen but not physically present, like a ghost.

Philander: to engage in frequent casual sex.

Philanthropy: a lover of human-kind, to make efforts for the betterment of.

Philosophy: the study of ideas.

Philtrum: the curved part of the upper lip below the nose.

Phoenix: a mythical bird that reincarnates from its own ashes.

Pianissimo: softly, as in music.

Piquant: pleasantly aromatic.

Pirouette: ballet technique involving spinning.

Pizzicato: play (violin etc) by plucking the strings rather than bowing.

Placid: calm, peaceful.

Plumage: a birds suit of feathers.

Pluvial: rainfall.

Pococurante: indifferent.

Poignant: touching in a sad way.

Ponceau: a bright red or reddish orange.

Porcelain: durable ceramic glaze, often decorative.

Portfolio: case for carrying documents.

Portico: roofed structure at entrance to a building.

Portmanteaux: large suitcases, or a new word formed by combining others.

Prairillon: grassy plain.

Precocious: early maturation.

Prelude: preliminary.

Preterlabent: flowing beside, as in a river.

Prismatic: the separation of light into a rainbow, as through a prism.

Pristine: in it original state.

Promethean: a defiant creative genius who does not care for critics.

Propinquity: close by, near.

Proscenium: the section of a stage in front of the curtain.

Prosody: the rhythm and intonation of a person's speech.

Provocative: to provoke or incite.

Prurient: lustful.

Psithurisma: a whispering sound, like the wind through trees.

Psittacism: speaking in tongues, automatic speech.

Psyche: the entire mind, both unconscious and conscious.

Punchinello: fat clown.

Puree: to render something into a smooth consistency.

Purlicue: the area between thumb and forefinger.

Pyrrhic: a victory achieved at very high cost.

Q

Quaquaversal: radiating out in all directions, like a star hanging in space.

Querencia: the place where the bull makes its stand in the bull ring.

Quintessence: the fifth element, or finest essence.

Quisquose: difficult to deal with.

Quiver: to shake or tremble.

Quotidian: occurring every day.

R

Radii: the plural form of radius, a line drawn from the centre of a circle to the edge.

Rapture: ecstasy, extreme happiness.

Rariora: collector's items, often rare and unusual.

Ravel: to weave or knit together.

Ratatouille: vegetable stew.

Realm: a royal domain, or simply any large property.

Recherché: sophisticated.

Recidivist: repeat offender.

Reciprocity: mutual interdependence of action.

Redivivus: revived, restored to life.

Redolent: an evocative odour.

Regalia: the trappings of royalty (i.e. badges, crests, banners etc).

Relinquish: to voluntarily give.

Reliquary: safe storage for holy relics (i.e. bones of saints).

Renaissance: rebirth, revival.

Repartee: swift and witty banter.

Replica: a copy.

Resonance: reverberation, harmonious echoes.

Resplendent: impressive sight.

Revenant: ghost, doppelganger.

Reverie: day-dream.

Rhapsody: inspired passion.

Rimulose: surface with small cracks or fissures.

Risorgimento: regrouping, re-organisation.

Roseate: rose-colored.

Roué: male sex-addict.

Rupestrian: made of rock, shaped by rock.

S

Sable: ferret-like animal prized for its dark fur.

Salient: leading, prominent.

Saline: salty.

Salubrious: healthy, promoting good health.

Salve: soothing, restorative lotion.

Sangfroid: cold-blood, cool under pressure.

Sanguine: optimism, or reddish-brown (blood coloured), .

Sapience: calm rationality, wisdom.

Sapphire: bright blue gemstone.

Sardonyx: variety of onyx (semi precious gem stone).

Satellite: orbiting body, as in the moon around the earth, earth around the sun.

Scarlet: bright-red.

Scepter: ceremonial rod, symbol of regal authority.

Schadenfreude: damaged joy (in German), pleasure in another's misfortune.

Schefflera: variety of tropical shrub grown for its colourful foliage.

Scialytic: shining light in the shadows.

Scilicet: namely, that is.

Scintilla: a very small thing, smaller than a jot.

Scion: the heir of a noble or wealth y family.

Sclera: the white of the eyes.

Scoliosis: abnormal curvature of the spine.

Scythe: sharp, crescent-shaped cutting blade used for harvesting.

Seizure: sudden gripping, taking hold of, epileptic fit.

Selcouth: unusual.

Selenian: of the moon.

Semblance: having the appearance of, though not necessarily real.

Semiotician: one who practices semiotics, the study of signs and symbols.

Sempiternal: eternal.

Senescence: growing old.

Sentient: conscious intelligence.

Sequacious: the order in which a series of events occurs.

Sequence: a series of events.

Sequester: to put away or hide in a safe place out of sight.

Seraglio: harem.

Seraphim: six-winged angel.

Serenade: a romantic song, often sung during courtship.

Serendipity: good fortune.

Serenity: calmness.

Sesquipedalian: given to using long words with many syllables.

Sestina: poem with six six-line stanzas.

Seven: the number following six.

Sforzando: strongly accented note, in music.

Sfumato: a drawing technique, like smoke, an image is formed without defining lines.

Shadow: negative image formed behind object by shining light on the object.

Shallow: not deep, superficial.

Shimmer: flickering light.

Shiver: to tremble.

Shrivel: to dry out and shrink.

Sibilant: hissing sound.

Sibyl: female fortune-teller.

Sidereal: relating to the stars.

Sidle: to walk in a furtive or oblique way.

Sienna: brownish clay.

Sierra: mountains.

Sigil: magic symbol or seal.

Silence: no sound.

Silhouette: portrait in outline only, solid black in-fill.

Silkscreen: method of printing images on fabric using silk stretched across a frame.

Tristiloquy: sad speech.

Silver: a noble metal, or shiny grey colour.

Simplicity: being simple.

Simulacrum: image that misrepresents reality.

Sinecure: easy job with little or no responsibility.

Siphon: to draw liquid through a tube using gravity.

Sirocco: hot south/south-easterly Mediterranean wind coming from Sahara.

Sisyphean: relating to Sisyphus, endless labour.

Sittella: type of flocking songbird.

Sleep: restful, restorative unconsciousness.

Slender: thin.

Slice: a carved piece of something, often not very thick.

Slither: to glide like a snake.

Sluice: water-channel, complete with regulator valve.

Smoulder: burn without flame.

Sobriquet: nickname.

Soigné: elegant.

Sojourn: brief visit.

Solace: consolation.

Solecism: an ungrammatical expression.

Solemn: dignified and serious.

Soliloquy: monologue, usually in context of dramatic performance.

Solipsism: the belief that one's own mind is the only one that surely exists.

Solstice: twice a year event Sun reaches highest position as seen from the Poles.

Sommelier: wine waiter.

Sonata: series of three solo musical compositions.

Sonnet: a poem with fourteen lines.

Soothe: to calm, or make feel better.

Sorcerer: practitioner of the magical arts.

Sotto voce: under-tone, quiet voice.

Soubrette: sassy woman character in a comedy.

Soufflé: baked dish of light consistency.

Sough: gentle sigh.

Souvenir: something found and kept.

Specious: appearing to be correct when in fact incorrect.

Spinal: of the spine.

Spiral: helix, a shape occurring frequently in Nature.

Splice: to weave together, as in two pieces of rope.

Spool: a wheel-like dispenser of tape, film or string.

Stasis: equilibrium.

Stiletto: small dagger, or kind of heel on woman's shoe.

Stillicide: overflow water from roof-guttering.

Sublime: beyond interpretation, very fine.

Succinct: brief and to the point.

Succor: to give assistance.

Suffuse: a gradual spreading, usually of light or liquid.

Suicide: to terminate one's own life.

Surreptitious: stealthy, secret.

Sussurant: a low, indistinct sound.

Svelte: slender, lithe, like a young woman.

Swain: a young, often amorous man.

Swath: a fan-like cut made by a scythe (i.e. cutting wheat).

Swerve: to deviate suddenly (i.e. he swerved to miss a dog).

Sweven: premonition, vision.

Swoon: to faint, lose consciousness.

Syllable: a single sound that together with others forms a word.

Sylph: graceful, slim young woman.

Sylvan: relating to a forest.

Symbiosis: two or more organisms living together for mutual benefit.

Symphony: series of orchestral movements.

Symposium: conference, often on academic topics.

Synchronicity: when two or more similar but apparently unconnected events occur.

Synecdoche: figure of speech in which a part is made to represent the whole or vice versa.

Syzygy: A series of two or more connected or corresponding things.

T

Tableaux: an artwork made up of carefully arranged elements.

Tacenda: matters not for discussion, tacitly ignored.

Taciturn: uncommunicative.

Talisman: good luck charm, protection against evil or harm.

Tapestry: woven decorative wall-hanging, often depicting a narrative of events.

Teleology: study of a phenomena in terms of its purpose rather than its cause.

Tellurian: earthly.

Tenuous: loose or weak in nature, as in a tenuous grip.

Tercet: in poetry, a series of three lines.

Terpsichorean: relating to the art of dance.

Tessellation: the careful juxtaposition of shapes in a pattern.

Tête-à-tête: head-to-head, a private conversation.

Theophany: direct experience of the divine presence.

Thionine: a reddish dye used to stain samples for microscopic viewing.

Threnody: a song or speech in praise of a deceased person.

Thylacine: Tasmanian Tiger (extinct).

Tintinnabulation: a tinkling sound.

Tilt: to slop, not level.

Tintinnabulation: the ringing of bells.

Tiramisu: coffee-flavoured desert.

Tolutiloquent: rapid speech.

Torrential: a torrent (of rain), very heavy flow.

Tourmaline: multi-coloured gemstone.

Traipse: to walk about, often aimlessly.

Tranquility: calm, peaceful.

Transience: brief, not lasting long.

Tregetour: theatrical magician.

Tremulous: trembling, shaking (as in being timid).

Trillium: a three-lobed white or scarlet flower.

Trinity: a group of three inter-related entities, forming a whole.

Triptych: art-work in three sections, each section expressing an aspect of a single theme.

Triste: sadness.

Tryst: a secret meeting (as between illicit lovers).

Turquoise: vivid blue-green colour.

U

Ubiquitous: present everywhere, or apparently so.

Ultramarine: vivid blue-purple.

Umbrage: take offence, be insulted.

Umbrella: portable canopy for protection against sun and rain.

V

Vaccinate: inoculate (confer immunity).

Vacillate: hesitate or waver over a decision.

Vacivity: space, as in a vacancy.

Vacuity: vacuum, absence of substance.

Valance: ornamental drape on a table top.

Vale: this earthly life; or farewell (from this life).

Valiant: brave, courageous.

Vanilla: flavoured by the vanilla bean; generic or bland.

Vaticinate: prediction, prophecy.

Vaudeville: form of musical theatre common in 19th Century.

Velleity: whimsical desire.

Vellum: long-lasting writing surface made from fine-grained leather.

Velvet: soft, luxurious cloth used for clothes, drapes etc.

Veneer: surface layer, often not very thick, perhaps hiding what lies beneath.

Venial: minor sin, one which may be readily forgiven.

Ventriloquist: entertainer who projects their voice into a puppet.

Veracity: truth.

Veranda: covered porch that provides cool, liveable space in hot climates.

Verisimilitude: the appearance of truth.

Vernal: relating to spring.

Verve: with style and flourish, spirited.

Vespertine: relating to evening.

Vestibule: transitional space inside the front door, leading into building proper.

Vestigial: a remnant of an earlier, larger structure (eg the human appendix).

Vesuviate: to erupt volcanically (like Mt Vesuvius).

Vetanda: taboo subjects.

Vexation: annoyance, anger.

Vicennial: occurring every twenty years.

Viceroy: governor, royal representative.

Vicious: relating to vice, or sin.

Vicissitudes: changes to circumstances, often for the worse.

Victuals: food, provisions.

Videlicet: namely.

Vigesimal: based on the number 20.

Vignette: a short story or sketch.

Villain: the antagonist, or 'baddie' in a dramatic story.

Vincible: vulnerable to harm.

Vinyl: a general purpose synthetic material often used in place of leather.

Viola: similar to violin, but larger and so with lower pitch.

Violet: deep purple.

Violin: stringed instrument, smaller than a viola. Played with a bow.

Viridian: blue-green, often used to describe the colour of tropic ocean.

Virtuoso: an accomplished master at a skill, literally to have virtue.

Vis-à-vis: face to face.

Visceral: relating to the intestines, often called 'gut-feel'.

Vista: view.

Visurient: desire excited by the sight of something.

Vitiate: impair, to make worse.

Vivacity: aliveness, high-spirits.

Vivify: invigorate.

Vivisepulture: to be buried alive.

Vociferous: loudly talkative.

Voluminous: large volume or amount.

W

Wan: pale (of complexion).

Warble: a high-pitched trill, as in a bird call.

Weather: atmospheric conditions.

Whilom: former.

Whimsy: an impulsive and possibly silly idea.

Whisper: to speak softly, often in a conspirational way.

Winceyette: cotton cloth.

Winnow: to separate the wheat from the chaff.

Wisteria: climbing, decorative plant with purple flowers.

Wyvern: legless dragon, snake-like.

X

Xenodochial: hospitable to strangers.

Xenoglossy: spontaneous language, not learned.

Xysti: covered entry to a gymnasium.

Y

Yowl: a wolf-like howl.

Z

Zenith: the highest point.

Zephyr: gentle breeze.

Zitella: unmarried woman.

Zyzzyva: weevil.

About the Author

Become friends with David Tuffley on Facebook:
http://www.facebook.com/tuffley/

www.ingramcontent.com/pod-product-compliance
Lightning Source LLC
Chambersburg PA
CBHW020355290526
45785CB00005B/2297